S0-BJQ-117

Jesus

Written by
Mary Elizabeth Tebo, FSP

Illustrated by
Mary Joseph Peterson, FSP

Illustrator Assistant
Laura Rosemarie McGowan, FSP

Pauline
BOOKS & MEDIA
Boston

Nihil Obstat:
Reverend Thomas W. Buckley, S.T.D., S.S.L.

Imprimatur:
✠ Seán Cardinal O'Malley, OFM, Cap.
Archbishop of Boston

June 23, 2008

Library of Congress Cataloging-in-Publication Data

Tebo, Mary Elizabeth.
 My first book about Jesus / written by Mary Elizabeth Tebo ; illustrated by
Mary Joseph Peterson ; illustrator assistant, Laura Rosemarie McGowan.
    p. cm.
 ISBN 0-8198-4865-4
 1. Jesus Christ--Person and offices--Juvenile literature. I. Peterson, Mary Joseph.
II. McGowan, Laura Rosemarie. III. Title.
 BT203.T43 2008
 232--dc22

                          2008023717

Published by Pauline Books & Media, 50 Saint Pauls Avenue,
Boston, MA 02130–3491.

Printed in U.S.A.

www.pauline.org

Pauline Books & Media is the publishing house of the Daughters of St. Paul,
an international congregation of women religious serving the Church with the
communications media.

1 2 3 4 5 6 7 8 9   12 11 10 09 08

PART ONE

THE LIFE OF JESUS

The Bible Tells Us about Jesus

The Bible is a very special book. It tells the story of God's love for all his people. God's plan was that we would live in friendship with him and enjoy the beautiful world he had created. But when the first man and woman disobeyed God, they broke this friendship. God promised that one day he would send us a Savior. After many, many years, God the Father sent his Son to earth. His name is Jesus, and he came to free us from our sinfulness.

God inspired certain people to write down the story of Jesus. We can read about many things that Jesus did and said in the books of the Bible that we call the Gospels.

Mary Says "Yes" to God

A long time ago there was a young woman named Mary. She lived in the land of Israel. Mary loved God very much. One day an angel named Gabriel came and stood by her.

"Mary," Gabriel greeted her, "God has chosen you to be the mother of his Son."

"How can this happen?" Mary asked in surprise.

"The Holy Spirit will come to you," Gabriel told her.

Mary closed her eyes and said, "Yes. I want to do whatever God asks of me."

"I have more good news for you, Mary," the angel Gabriel continued. "Your cousin Elizabeth is going to have a baby, too!"

When the angel had left, Mary thought for a long time. The angel had brought her such wonderful, unexpected news. She knew her life would change forever....

Jesus Is Born in Bethlehem

The Roman emperor called for a census. All the people had to return to their hometowns to be counted. So Mary and her husband, Joseph, prepared their little donkey for the long trip to Bethlehem.

When they reached Bethlehem, Joseph began to worry. There were so many people there that Joseph and Mary couldn't find a place to stay.

"You must be looking for shelter," said a friendly man who had been watching them knock on door after door. "You can stay in a cave not far from here. I'll show you the way."

Mary and Joseph followed the kind stranger to the cave. That very night, Jesus was born!

Angels appeared, singing, and they told
some shepherds about the newborn baby.
The shepherds hurried to the cave. They
saw Mary and Joseph and Baby Jesus. It
was a joyful night!

Mary and Joseph Present Jesus to God

Some time later Joseph and Mary took Jesus to the Temple in Jerusalem. They wanted to present him to God.

A holy man named Simeon was praying in the Temple at that very moment. He was very happy when he saw the baby in Mary's arms.

Simeon prayed, "O God, now I have seen your salvation. This child will be a light to all people."

There was also a holy woman named Anna in the Temple. She praised God, too, when she saw Baby Jesus.

Joseph and Mary were amazed at everything they heard. They wondered what little Jesus would say and do when he grew up.

The Holy Family
Flees into Egypt

One night Joseph had a frightening dream. An angel warned him that the town of Bethlehem was no longer safe. King Herod had heard about Baby Jesus. Wise men from the East had told him that Jesus was a newborn king. Herod was afraid that Jesus would take his place as ruler. Herod's soldiers were out looking for Jesus.

"You must escape this very night!" the angel told Joseph.

Joseph woke up with a start. Quickly he prepared their little donkey for another journey. They left while it was still night to escape danger. Joseph took Mary and Jesus to faraway Egypt, where they lived until it was safe to return to Israel. Then they settled in the town of Nazareth.

Life with Mary and Joseph

After such an exciting beginning, the Bible doesn't tell us much about Jesus as a child. In fact, we don't learn anything else about him until he turns twelve years old! But Jesus was probably very much like other children his age—playing with friends, helping his parents, and learning new things. Sometimes Mary must have asked him to help her with simple tasks. He might have collected wood for the fire or helped her to draw water from the well. Joseph worked as a carpenter. We know that Jesus learned to be a carpenter, too. Mary and Joseph would have made sure that Jesus also learned about their Jewish faith. He learned to pray and to read the Scriptures. All this helped to prepare him for the mission that his heavenly Father had given him....

Jesus Stays behind in the Temple

When Jesus was twelve years old, his family made their usual trip to Jerusalem to celebrate the Jewish feast of Passover. After the celebration, the family left the city with their relatives and friends. Soon Mary and Joseph discovered that Jesus was missing. What could have happened to him?

Three long days went by, but Mary and Joseph couldn't find Jesus anywhere. Finally they decided to search the Temple.

There they saw Jesus. He was talking with the teachers in the Temple.

Mary ran up to her son and hugged him tight.

"Jesus! We've looked everywhere for you! Why have you done this?"

"Didn't you know I would be in my Father's house?" Jesus asked.

Mary and Joseph were puzzled by Jesus' answer, but they didn't ask him what he meant. They were just happy to have found him safe and sound!

Jesus Meets John the Baptist

Many years passed, and Jesus grew up. Soon Jesus would begin the mission that God the Father had given to him.

One day Jesus went to the river Jordan. He saw his cousin, John, who was baptizing and preaching to the people.

"You must be sorry for your sins and turn back to God," John told the people.

Jesus also went to the river to be baptized. At first John, knowing who Jesus was, asked to be baptized by Jesus! Then John understood this was the way God wanted it. So Jesus stepped into the river and John baptized him, pouring water over him.

Suddenly, John heard a mysterious voice: "This is my Son, whom I love very much."

And he saw the Holy Spirit come to Jesus, appearing as a snowy-white dove.

John was amazed and began to tell many people about Jesus.

Jesus Calls His Followers

When Jesus began his mission to teach about the kingdom of God, he decided to choose twelve special followers. They would be his apostles. He would teach the apostles, and they would be able to teach others about our loving Father in heaven.

Some of the apostles were fisherman. While Jesus was walking along the shore of a very large lake one day, he saw Peter, Andrew, James, and John. They were in their fishing boats.

"Follow me," Jesus said. "Together we will fish for people!"

So they left their boats and their nets and the fish they had caught and followed Jesus. Later Jesus asked eight other men to be his special followers. Their names were Philip; Bartholomew; Matthew; Thomas; another man called James; Simon; Judas, the son of James; and Judas Iscariot.

The Wedding at Cana

One day Mary, the mother of Jesus, was invited to a wedding. Jesus and some of his friends were also invited. During the feast Mary noticed that the wine was running out. If that happened, the celebration would be ruined!

Mary had an idea. She whispered to her son, "Jesus! They have no more wine."

Jesus smiled at his Mother. "What can I do?" he said. "It's not my time yet."

But Mary knew he would help. She went to the servants and said, "Do whatever Jesus tells you!"

So Jesus told them to fill stone jars full of water. When they had filled them, the servants couldn't believe their eyes! The water had turned into wine! And it was even more delicious than the first wine had been.

This was Jesus' first miracle.

Jesus Teaches People

After this, Jesus began to travel around the country, teaching people about the kingdom of God. Often he told stories to help people understand what he meant. He said that the kingdom of God is like a tiny mustard seed. It's so small you would barely notice it. But if you plant it in the ground, it can become a wonderful tree. Even the birds could enjoy perching in its branches!

Jesus also said that the kingdom of God is like a marvelous buried treasure or a perfect pearl. To have God's love growing within us—and to share God's love with others—is the most amazing treasure we could ever discover.

Jesus Heals a Paralyzed Man

One day Jesus was teaching in Peter's house. It was crowded with people.

Some men came, carrying a man who could not walk. "We need to see Jesus!" they said.

No one moved to let them near.

They said to each other, "Let's climb up to the roof."

Before long, the men carefully lowered their friend into the room—through a hole in the roof. The crowd watched in surprise.

Jesus said to the paralyzed man, "Your sins are forgiven."

"But only
God can forgive
sins!" someone said.

Jesus turned to the man
lying on his cot and said, "Get up and
walk. You are healed."

The man got up and stood straight and
tall before the crowd. How could he thank
Jesus?

"Return to your home," Jesus said to
him.

The man left, full of joy.

Jesus Walks on the Water

One evening, after teaching the crowds all day long, Jesus said to his friends, "Row to the other side of the lake. I will send the crowds home."

So Jesus' friends got into Peter's boat and left. But in the middle of the night there was a terrible storm.

The boat began to sink! Then Jesus' friends saw something amazing. It looked like Jesus. He was walking toward them— on the waves!

Jesus called out, "It's me. Don't be afraid!"

Peter replied, "Lord, let me come to you!"

"Come!" Jesus replied. Peter got out of the boat. But the waves were very powerful. Soon he grew afraid.

"Help me!" he cried.

Jesus caught Peter's arm. Together they climbed into the boat.

The wind died down, and the water became calm again.

The Transfiguration

One day Jesus took Peter, James, and John and climbed up a mountain.

When they reached the top, Jesus began to pray. Suddenly, his clothes began to shine and looked as white as snow. Then Elijah the prophet and Moses both appeared. They spoke to Jesus!

Peter, James, and John watched in amazement. A cloud fell upon them, and they heard a voice say, "This is my Son, whom I love."

Peter, James, and John hid their faces. When it was quiet, they looked around. There was no one else there except Jesus. His clothes were no longer bright and shining.

As they climbed down the mountain, Jesus said to Peter, James, and John, "Don't tell anyone about this until I rise from the dead."

Jesus Enters Jerusalem

The feast of Passover was near. Jesus and his friends went to Jerusalem for this special celebration. One of Jesus' friends borrowed a donkey for Jesus to ride. They spread a cloak on the donkey's back, and the donkey carried Jesus into the great city of Jerusalem.

Many people who had heard Jesus teaching were also in the city for the Passover. When the crowds saw that Jesus was coming, they welcomed him with joy.

They shouted, "Praise God!"

Some people picked big leafy branches off nearby trees. They laid the branches on the road for the donkey to walk on. It was like a royal welcome!

Then Jesus went to the Temple.

The Last Supper

Jesus and his friends celebrated the Passover meal together. Jesus knew that one of his friends was going to betray him. He knew that this was the last time he would celebrate this feast with his friends. So on this night, Jesus gave his friends a very special gift....

Jesus thanked his Father for the bread and the wine that they were about to eat and drink. Then he gave them to his friends. He told them that he was giving them his very own body and blood to eat and drink. This was the gift of the Eucharist! He asked his apostles to celebrate this meal often. Even though Jesus was saying good-bye to his friends, he didn't want to leave them alone. He would always be with them.

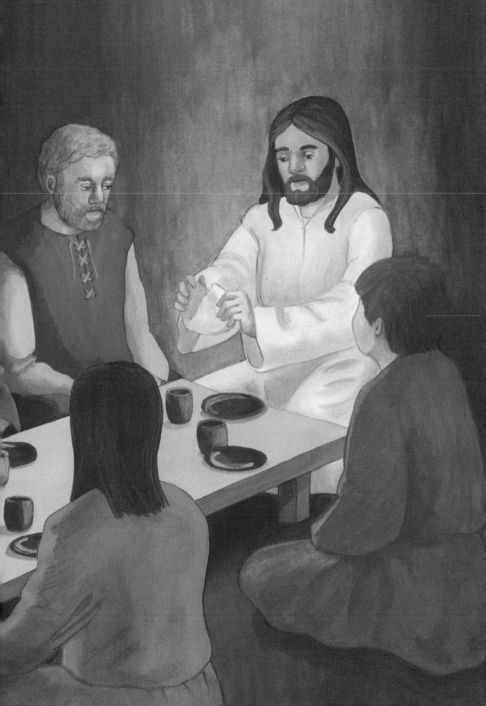

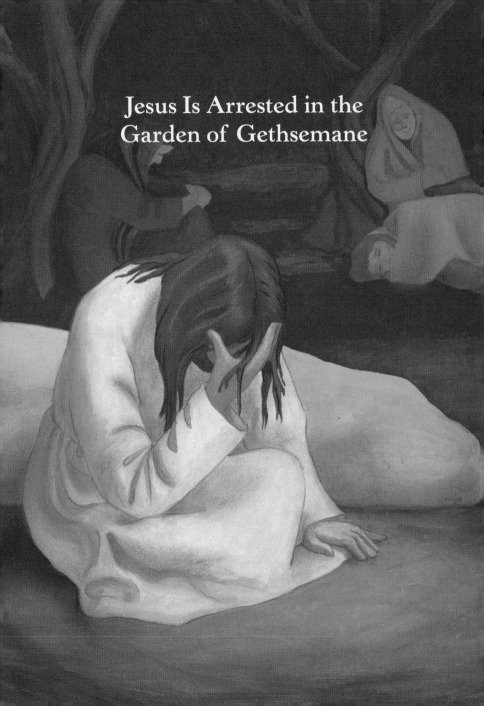

Jesus Is Arrested in the
Garden of Gethsemane

After they had finished the Passover meal, Jesus and his friends walked to a garden called Gethsemane. Jesus liked to pray there. This night, he felt very afraid. Judas Iscariot had gone to betray him. Jesus asked Peter, James, and John to pray with him. Then he knelt down.

"My Father," he prayed, "help me to do your will."

After a while, Jesus got up to talk to Peter. But Peter and the others had fallen fast asleep! Jesus woke them up and again asked them to pray with him. Then he began to pray to his Father once more. Meanwhile, Peter, James, and John tried to stay awake. But, one by one, they each dropped off to sleep once more.

Soon soldiers arrived at the garden. They were looking for Jesus. Judas had led them to him. They arrested Jesus and took him away.

Jesus Carries the Cross

The soldiers brought Jesus to the governor, Pontius Pilate.

He asked Jesus, "Is it true that you are a king?"

Jesus quietly answered, "If I had an earthly kingdom, my subjects would be here to defend me, wouldn't they?"

Pontius Pilate was confused. Jesus didn't seem like a criminal, but some people said that he was. Pilate didn't want to cause a riot.

So he gave the crowd a choice: "I will let one prisoner go free today. Shall I free Barabbas or Jesus?"

The people who didn't like Jesus yelled, "Barabbas!"

So Pilate ordered that Jesus must die. Jesus carried a heavy cross all the way to the hill called Golgotha. A stranger named Simon from Cyrene helped Jesus.

Jesus Dies on the Cross

When they reached Golgotha, the soldiers put Jesus on the cross. They also crucified two criminals. One of them made fun of Jesus. But the other knew that Jesus had not done anything wrong.

"You will share in the kingdom of God," Jesus promised him.

Jesus' mother, Mary, found her way to the front of the crowd. She wanted to stand near her son. Jesus' friend, the apostle John, was with her. The other apostles had been too frightened to face the crowd. But John stayed close to Mary. Jesus was grateful that his mother wasn't alone on this very sad day.

Jesus prayed to his Father, saying, "Father, I put my life in your hands." Then he died.

41

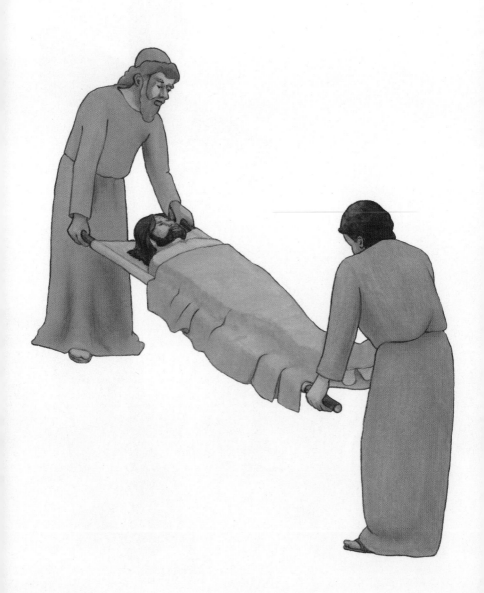

The Burial of Jesus

Joseph, from the town of Arimathea, asked Pontius Pilate for permission to bury Jesus. Another of Jesus' followers, Nicodemus, brought spices for the burial. They carefully took Jesus down from the cross. They wrapped his body in linen and placed it in a new tomb in a garden. Some of the women who had also followed Jesus paid attention to where Jesus was buried so they could return after the Sabbath celebration.

Mary Magdalene sat and watched as Joseph rolled the huge stone in front of Jesus' tomb. She missed Jesus very much. Then the women returned to Jerusalem. There was nothing they could do now except wait.

Jesus Rises from the Dead

After the Sabbath, Mary Magdalene went to Jesus' tomb in the garden. It was early morning and still dark outside, but

she could see that the stone had been rolled away. Looking inside, she discovered that Jesus' body wasn't there! *Who could have taken his body?* she wondered.

She told Peter and the others the news. They discovered that Mary was right—the body of Jesus was gone!

Mary sat on the ground and began to cry. This was terrible! Just then, she heard a sound behind her. *It must be the gardener,* she thought. She would ask him about Jesus.

"Did *you* take him away, sir?"

But the man just smiled at her and said, "Mary!"

Mary jumped to her feet. She recognized his voice. It was Jesus! He was alive!

"Mary, tell my friends that I am going to my Father," Jesus said.

Mary ran as fast as she could to spread the wonderful news!

The Disciples Meet Jesus on the Road to Emmaus

That evening, two of Jesus' disciples walked to the town of Emmaus. A stranger joined them on the road.

"What are you talking about?" the stranger asked.

"Haven't you heard the terrible news?" they replied in disbelief.

"What news?" the stranger asked.

"Jesus was killed. We thought that he would save Israel," they responded sadly.

"You must not understand what is written in God's Word," the stranger replied. He began to explain God's Word to them.

When night fell, the disciples invited him to join them for supper. They sat down to eat, and their guest blessed the bread and broke it. In a flash, the disciples realized that this stranger was really Jesus himself! But just as they recognized him, he disappeared. They were so happy. They got up and hurried back to Jerusalem to tell the others!

"We have seen the Lord!" they cried, as they burst into the room.

"Peter has seen him, too! It's true—he has risen!" the other disciples exclaimed.

Jesus Returns to the Father

While the disciples were eating supper, Jesus appeared in the room with them.

"Don't be afraid," he said. "It's me!"

Jesus' friends looked at him in surprise.

So Jesus asked, "May I have something to eat, too?"

Someone offered Jesus a plate of fish, and he ate it. Everyone was amazed.

Jesus remained forty days with his friends, teaching them and answering their questions. Then, on the fortieth day, they all walked up a large hill.

Jesus blessed his friends and reminded them that he would be with them forever. He asked them to continue his mission by teaching people everywhere about the kingdom of God.

As Jesus rose up to heaven, he said, "I am going back to the Father. Return to the city, and wait for the Holy Spirit."

PART TWO

JESUS IS WITH US ALWAYS

Jesus Gives His Spirit
to the Disciples

Jesus' friends went to the upper room where they had stayed since the Last Supper. They prayed and sang and waited for the Holy Spirit to come. Mary, Jesus' mother, stayed with them, too.

On the Feast of Pentecost, something amazing happened while they were praying. There was a great roar of wind in their tiny room. Flames of fire seemed to appear from heaven and rest on each one of them. They received the gifts of the Holy Spirit to help them spread the Good News of Jesus around the world. The disciples discovered that they were no longer afraid. They were full of joy and began to speak about Jesus to everyone they met.

The Church Is
the Body of Christ

Pentecost marked the beginning of the Church. When Jesus returned to the Father, he promised that he would always be with us, until the end of the world. Even though we can't see him or talk to him face to face like the apostles did, we believe that Jesus keeps his promise to us.

Jesus remains with us in a special way through the Church, which continues his mission of teaching people the Good News of God's love. This is why we call the Church the Body of Christ.

Jesus is with us in a special way through the seven sacraments....

Jesus Gives Us His Life:
Baptism, Confirmation,
and Eucharist

Through the sacraments of Baptism, Confirmation, and Eucharist, we become followers of Jesus.

Baptism is the very first sacrament we receive. It makes us part of the Church, the Body of Christ. This means that we are called to live as Jesus did, loving God and others.

Confirmation strengthens the gifts of the Holy Spirit within us. Just as the apostles became courageous and wanted to tell others about Jesus, the Holy Spirit helps us to live as good Christians every day.

The celebration of the Eucharist strengthens the life of God within us. When we receive Jesus in the Eucharist, we grow closer to God—and we grow closer to one another, too.

Jesus Heals Us: Reconciliation and the Anointing of the Sick

Jesus healed many people who were sick, and he forgave those who had sinned. Through the sacraments of Reconciliation and Anointing of the Sick, this work of Jesus is continued in the Church.

When we receive the sacrament of Reconciliation, we are asking God for forgiveness for the times we have sinned. The new life of God we received in baptism can grow again in our hearts.

When people are very sick, the Church anoints them with oil. The Church prays that the person who is sick will receive courage and peace from the Holy Spirit. This sacrament is a sign that God is with us even during very difficult times.

Jesus Helps Us Love One Another: Holy Orders and Matrimony

These two sacraments, Holy Orders and Matrimony, help us to follow Jesus more closely. Unlike the other sacraments, not everyone receives Holy Orders or Matrimony. God calls each person to a different vocation in life. Through our vocations, we grow more like Jesus by our service to others.

A man whom God calls to receive Holy Orders becomes a deacon or a priest. He is called to show his love for God by helping others. He does this especially through the celebration of the sacraments and by teaching about the Word of God.

Many people are called by God to the sacrament of Matrimony. Through this sacrament, a man and a woman promise to love each other for their entire lives. Their love for each other and their family is a sign to the world of God's love for us.

We Pray Like Jesus: The Our Father

We stay close to Jesus by praying every day.

When Jesus' friends asked him how they should pray, Jesus taught them a special prayer to our heavenly Father. We call this prayer the Our Father.